SCIENCE
VS
CRIME

by Angela Royston

Raintree is an imprint of Capstone Global Library Limited, a company incorporated in England and Wales having its registered office at 264 Banbury Road, Oxford OX2 7DY – Registered company number: 6695582

www.raintree.co.uk
myorders@raintree.co.uk

Text © Capstone Global Library Limited 2016
The moral rights of the proprietor have been asserted.

Produced for Raintree by Calcium
Edited by Sarah Eason and Amanda Learmonth
Designed by Simon Borrough
Picture research by Rachel Blount
Production by Victoria Fitzgerald
Originated by Capstone Global Library © 2016
Printed and bound in China

ISBN 978 1 4747 1614 7 (hardback)
19 18 17 16 15
10 9 8 7 6 5 4 3 2 1

ISBN 978 1 4747 1620 8 (paperback)
20 19 18 17 16
10 9 8 7 6 5 4 3 2 1

British Library Cataloguing in Publication Data
A full catalogue record for this book is available from the British Library.

Acknowledgements
We would like to thank the following for permission to reproduce photographs: Dreamstime: 18percentgrey 35, 36clicks 28, Amaviael 36, Boazyiftach 26, Gtmedia 38, Kpanizza 23, Lcjtripod 39, Odvdveer 4, Photowitch 5, 45tr, Robcorbett 25, Showface 18, 20, 45tm, Soleg1974 32, Supersport 29, Svsphoto 31, Timnichols1956 34, Viktorus 42, Zarg40441; Shutterstock: Alexandru-Radu Borzea 17, Zbynek Burival 24, Kevin L Chesson 3, 16, 45bc, Corepics VOF 8, Paul Drabot 36–37, Edhar 14, Edw 9, 44, Elisanth 33, 45bl, Ragne Kabanova 10, Kilukilu 7, 12, Vit Kovalcik 21, Zlatko Guzmic 43, Mikeledray 27, Neokryuger 15, Olivier Le Queinec 10–11, 45tl, Loren Rodgers 6, Noel Powell, Schaumburg 22, Shock 30, Stocksolutions 40, Leah-Anne Thompson 13, 19.

Cover photographs reproduced with permission of: Shutterstock: Andrey Burmakin (tl), Loren Rodgers (br)

Every effort has been made to contact copyright holders of material reproduced in this book. Any omissions will be rectified in subsequent printings if notice is given to the publisher.

All the internet addresses (URLs) given in this book were valid at the time of going to press. However, due to the dynamic nature of the internet, some addresses may have changed, or sites may have changed or ceased to exist since publication. While the author and publisher regret any inconvenience this may cause readers, no responsibility for any such changes can be accepted by either the author or the publisher.

Some words are shown in bold, **like this**. You can find out what they mean by looking in the glossary.

Contents

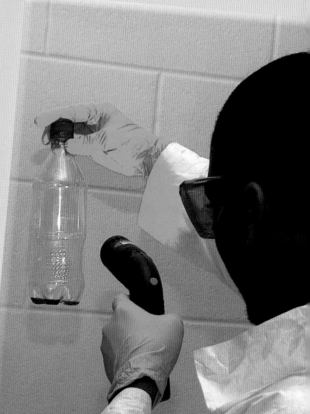

A world of crime

Crimes are being committed every minute of every day. They include all types of crime, from computer hacking to violent crimes against people. It is the job of the police not only to find the criminals, but also to produce evidence to prove they committed the crime. A court of law examines the evidence and decides whether or not a suspect is guilty.

THE CRIMES

Crimes hurt people in many different ways. Homicide and **assault** kill or injure. Most violent criminals use weapons such as guns or knives. Other crimes affect property. Thieves steal what does not belong to them, and may use violence to do so. Some criminals attack strangers, but many crimes are committed by people who know the victim.

SOLVING CRIMES

Some crimes are easy to solve. Criminals may give themselves up or confess. Criminals can even be killed as they carry out a crime, such as a robbery in which they are shot by the victim. If the victim knows the criminals, he or she can give the police valuable information. Other crimes are much harder to solve. When it is not clear who has committed a crime, the police may ask **forensic scientists** to help them. They also talk to **witnesses**, and the victim's friends and family. If they suspect a particular person, they look for evidence that links the suspect to the crime. They search the suspect's home and car, and check police files for any previous, similar crimes.

Security check
A security gate detects metal objects such as knives and guns. It prevents people from carrying hidden weapons onto aeroplanes.

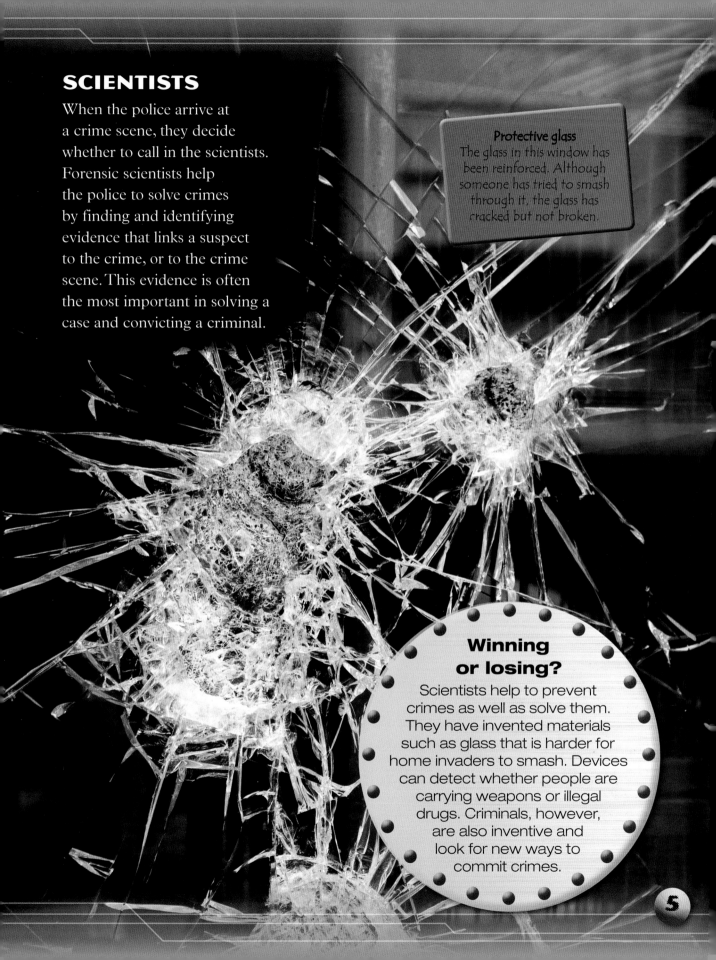

SCIENTISTS

When the police arrive at a crime scene, they decide whether to call in the scientists. Forensic scientists help the police to solve crimes by finding and identifying evidence that links a suspect to the crime, or to the crime scene. This evidence is often the most important in solving a case and convicting a criminal.

Protective glass
The glass in this window has been reinforced. Although someone has tried to smash through it, the glass has cracked but not broken.

Winning or losing?
Scientists help to prevent crimes as well as solve them. They have invented materials such as glass that is harder for home invaders to smash. Devices can detect whether people are carrying weapons or illegal drugs. Criminals, however, are also inventive and look for new ways to commit crimes.

Chapter one: Crime scene investigation

The crime scene is the place where the crime happened. It may be a house or flat that has been burgled, or the place where the body of a murdered person is found. It could be where the computers or mobile phones were used to commit fraud and other crimes. The crime scene is the most likely place for police and forensic scientists to find evidence. For that reason, it is important that nothing is disturbed.

Keeping out the public
The police seal off a crime scene with police tape. Only other officers and the forensic team can cross the tape.

POLICE LINE DO NOT CROSS

FIRST ON THE SCENE

The first police officer to arrive takes charge of the crime scene until a superior officer arrives. The first priority is to take care of anyone who is wounded. The second priority is to see whether the criminal is still there and detain him or her. The next step is to take the names and addresses of any witnesses. While all this is happening, however, it is vitally important that evidence is not lost or disturbed. If any evidence is touched or moved it can become changed or **contaminated**, and therefore unusable in a court of law.

MORE THAN ONE CRIME SCENE

Some crimes involve several crime scenes. In a murder, for example, the attack might be committed in one place, and the body taken by car and buried somewhere else, creating three crime scenes.

Winning or losing?
Detectives are very careful not to disturb a crime scene or contaminate evidence. However, criminals have also become more careful. They know what kind of evidence could connect them to the crime scene. They wear gloves to cover their fingerprints and hoods so that they cannot be recognized.

Photographic evidence
This forensic photograph taken at the scene of a crime shows a gun and gun cartridges. The numbers help to identify them.

THE FORENSIC TEAM MOVES IN

A forensic team consists of several people, and each has their own job to do. The photographer is one of the first people to start work. He or she photographs every piece of evidence in the exact positions they are found. They also photograph the whole scene to show how the pieces of evidence fit together. Once something has been photographed, it can be examined more closely or taken to the forensic laboratory.

Searching for evidence

The forensic team first examine and record the most obvious evidence at a crime scene. They then examine the whole area. for smaller pieces of evidence, such as splashes of blood, which might help them to work out exactly what happened there.

DO NOT TOUCH!

When evidence is found, it is often first ringed with chalk and numbered before it is photographed. Each piece of evidence is then put into a plastic bag to prevent it from being contaminated. If fingerprint experts were later examining a gun for fingerprints, it would be disastrous if they found the detective's fingerprints on it. The police then could not prove that the detective was not the murderer!

Getting the picture
Forensic photographs have to be clear and exact. They may be used later in court to help to convict the suspect.

In the ring

Frenchman Alphonse Bertillon (1853–1914) was the first person to photograph a crime scene before it was disturbed. He photographed the whole scene and all the evidence, including the body, from every angle. He also photographed known criminals to identify them if they later reoffended.

FINGERTIP SEARCH

Outdoor crime scenes are difficult to search and may cover a large area. Police wear special suits so that their own hair or threads of clothing do not contaminate the area. Then they get down on their hands and knees and search every square centimetre of ground. They may use magnifying glasses, small brushes and other tools to help them. They pick up tiny scraps of evidence with tweezers and put each piece into a plastic bag.

Protective clothing
A plastic suit covers the forensic scientist from head to toe. The suit protects the evidence from contamination by the scientist.

Examining the body

In a murder case, the first question to be answered is how the victim died. Police and forensic scientists photograph and examine any cuts, gunshot wounds and other injuries. They then try to work out what position the murderer and the victim were in when the killing occurred. A forensic **pathologist** is a doctor who takes charge of the body.

The autopsy room
Bodies are examined by pathologists in a special place called an autopsy room. Everything there is kept spotlessly clean.

TIME OF DEATH

The next question to answer is at what time did the person die. It is almost impossible to tell this from the body alone. The sooner the body is discovered, however, the more accurately the pathologist can work out the time of death. Blood at the scene also gives some clues. How fresh it is shows how long ago the murder occurred. The amount of blood found also indicates how quickly the person died, because bleeding stops as soon as the heart stops beating.

MURDER OR SUICIDE?

Some murderers try to hide their crime by making it look as though the person killed themself. They may put a gun in the victim's hand. Investigators and pathologists work together to try to find the truth. They examine whether the bullet had been fired from that gun (see pages 26–27) and they work out where the gun must have been held before it was fired. They can then see if it was possible for the person to fire the gun themself.

AUTOPSY

When a body has been examined at the crime scene it is taken to the pathologist's lab. If the cause of death is not clear, the pathologist must examine the victim's organs. They look for traces of poison or drugs inside the person's stomach. They examine the lungs to see if the victim had been drowned or suffocated. They also check whether the person died of a heart attack or other natural cause.

Breaking through

Dutch scientists have invented a way for investigators to examine a crime scene. Instead of visiting the site themselves, they see it on a 3D videotape. The videotape is produced using two cameras that film every aspect of the crime scene. It also allows the investigators to bring photos of other objects onto the screen to compare them to those in the tape.

Footprints and other evidence

Criminals leave behind pieces of evidence, which give forensic scientists information. By comparing evidence found in different places, detectives can build up a more complete picture. For example, if a knife is found in the bushes, does it match the victim's wounds? When there is more than one crime scene, evidence found at each one helps detectives to work out who was present at each scene.

TREAD MARKS

Vehicle tyres and the soles of many shoes have treads, which vary with different brands. If a footprint matches the treads on one of the suspect's shoes, it does not prove that the suspect was at the crime scene – another person might have shoes with the same pattern. However, it adds weight to any other evidence found against the suspect.

Whose footprint?
A footprint found at the crime scene is examined and compared with all the suspect's shoes to see if it matches any of them.

SCRAPS OF EVIDENCE

Even tiny pieces of criminal evidence can be amazingly important. A bullet is fired when gunpowder in the barrel of the gun explodes. Tiny specks of gunpowder scatter after the shot and can cling to the shooter's clothes. This is important if suspects claim that they have never fired a gun, yet specks are found on their clothes. Similarly, specks of blood, hairs and threads of materials can all help to link a suspect to the crime scene. For example, does dirt found in the suspect's car match dirt at the crime scene?

Breaking through

Scientists can tell a lot from a single hair. If it is found on a suspect, it may be matched to the victim's hair. If it is found on the victim, it may be matched to the suspect. A lock of hair reveals even more. Scientists can now analyze a lock of hair and detect whether the person has been drinking alcohol or using drugs. The hair contains traces of these and other substances used during the three months before the crime.

A closer look
Forensic scientists examine suspect's clothing under a magnifying glass. They look for tiny specks of evidence, such as gunpowder or blood.

Chapter two: Personal markers

Everybody is unique. Everyone's face looks different and this is how we recognize the people we know. Some people look similar and many people change the way they look, but they cannot change some things. No one else, for example, has exactly the same pattern of ridges on the skin of their fingertips as you do. What makes each person unique is a substance in the body called **DNA**.

WHAT IS DNA?

To discover what DNA is you must venture into one of the trillions of tiny cells that make up your body. Cells are the building blocks for every part of the body. The skin, for example, is made of skin cells and the blood is made of blood cells. Each kind of cell has a different job to do, but each cell contains the same DNA. This DNA contains the **genes** you inherited from your parents, but in your DNA the combination of the genes is slightly different to that of your parents. DNA forms genes which control how each cell forms and grows.

A face in a crowd
Everyone has eyes, a nose and a mouth, but the shape and size of these and other features give you a unique appearance.

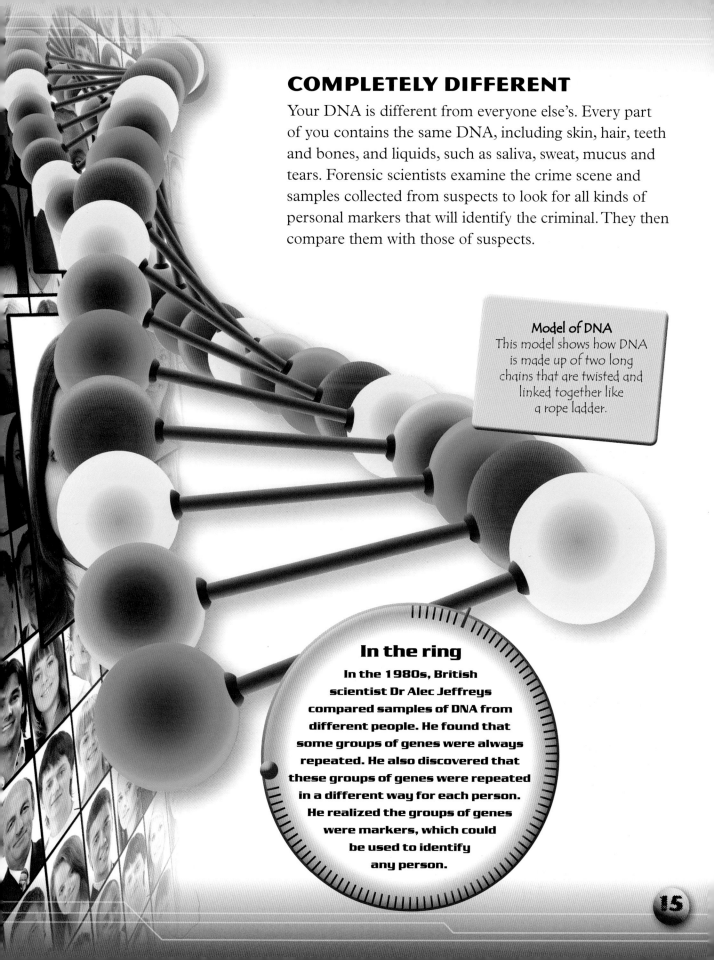

COMPLETELY DIFFERENT

Your DNA is different from everyone else's. Every part of you contains the same DNA, including skin, hair, teeth and bones, and liquids, such as saliva, sweat, mucus and tears. Forensic scientists examine the crime scene and samples collected from suspects to look for all kinds of personal markers that will identify the criminal. They then compare them with those of suspects.

Model of DNA
This model shows how DNA is made up of two long chains that are twisted and linked together like a rope ladder.

In the ring

In the 1980s, British scientist Dr Alec Jeffreys compared samples of DNA from different people. He found that some groups of genes were always repeated. He also discovered that these groups of genes were repeated in a different way for each person. He realized the groups of genes were markers, which could be used to identify any person.

Fingerprints

Whenever you touch a hard, smooth surface, you leave fingerprints on it. Detectives brush powder over any surfaces the criminal may have touched, such as door handles, weapons and tools found at the crime scene. Many of the prints will be smeared or confused with other prints. When a clear print is found, it is photographed or lifted onto sticky tape and examined later in the lab.

Hidden prints
Some fingerprint powders are fluorescent. This means they glow, or fluoresce, when a laser beam is shone on them.

FINGERPRINT PATTERNS

If you look carefully at the pads of flesh at the end of your fingers, you will see that the skin has many tiny lines or ridges, which form patterns. Some of the patterns remain the same throughout your life. They form three main shapes, called loops, whorls and arches.

Scientists use computer programmes to measure the exact shape of the patterns and the distances between the lines. The computer then compares them with the fingerprints of other people that have already been recorded.

PALM PRINTS TO IRISES

Fingerprints are not the only unique patterns in the human body. Toe prints and palm prints are too. In 1963, Lee Harvey Oswald was identified as the **assassin** of US President John F. Kennedy because his palm print matched that on the rifle used. Some prints can be compared by an expert using a magnifying glass, but computers are needed to compare other unique patterns in an individual. Most important in identification is the pattern of the iris, the coloured ring around the pupil of the eye.

In the ring

Fingerprints have been used for a long time in place of signatures by people who could not read or write. Sir Francis Galton (1822–1911) collected more than 8,000 sets of fingerprints and examined them in great detail. He worked out a system for classifying and comparing fingerprints of different people. His system has eight main categories and it is still used and accepted by the courts of law today.

Forensic testing

Prints taken at the scene of the crime are treated in the lab to get a clearer print, which can then be analyzed.

Blood and other fluids

Body fluids such as blood are often found at a crime scene. If the blood is still wet, a sample is collected on a swab and stored in an airtight container. If it has dried, some is scraped onto clean paper and bagged. There may be blood from different people at the crime scene, so it is important to keep each sample separate. The samples are taken to the laboratory for testing.

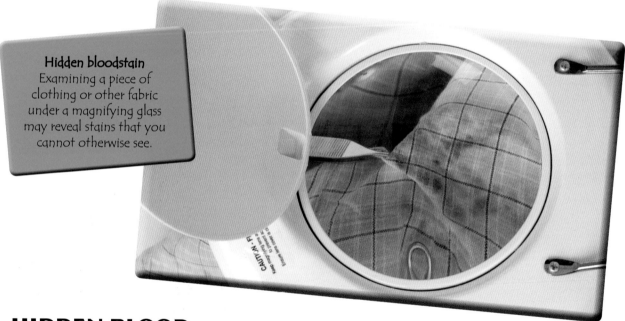

Hidden bloodstain
Examining a piece of clothing or other fabric under a magnifying glass may reveal stains that you cannot otherwise see.

HIDDEN BLOOD

In a violent crime, some of the victim's blood may splash the attacker's clothes. Most criminals throw away their bloodstained clothes, so police always search thoroughly in rubbish bins and elsewhere. Other criminals wash their clothes until the blood is no longer visible.

Forensic scientists can find the stains, however, with the help of a magnifying glass, but they have to test to make sure that the stains are blood. In one test, a chemical called **luminol** is sprayed onto the stain. If the stain contains even a tiny amount of blood, it shines with a blue light.

EXAMINING BLOOD

Everyone's blood is one of four basic groups, called A, B, O and AB. Different groups are most common in different parts of the world. For example, Group A is most common among Europeans, while group B is most common among Africans and Asians. Identifying which blood group a sample belongs to is helpful to forensic scientists, but blood is most useful as a source of DNA.

Swab test
A forensic scientist uses special chemical solutions to test for saliva, sweat and other fluids made by the body.

Breaking through

Using DNA to match blood or other samples found at a crime scene with a suspect has become increasingly common since 1987. Forensic scientists now also use DNA to identify people who are already dead. Although the DNA of everyone is unique, the DNA of members of the same family is very similar. Detectives identified the body of the terrorist leader Osama bin Laden by comparing his DNA with that of close family members.

Sampling DNA

Technology has improved so much in the last 20 years that smaller and smaller samples of DNA can now be analyzed. Forensic scientists collect DNA from tiny splashes of blood or from skin that was trapped under a victim's fingernails when he or she scratched his or her attacker.

Taking a DNA sample
DNA is collected by scraping a swab across the inside of the cheek. Police are suspicious if a suspect refuses to give a sample.

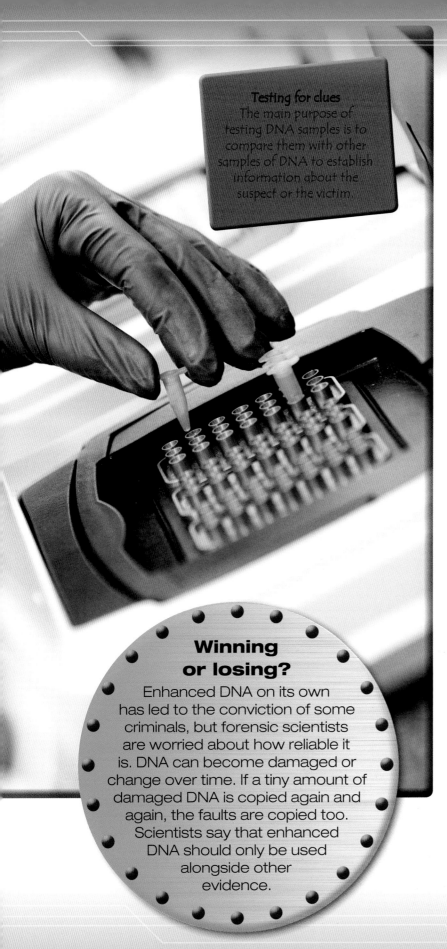

Testing for clues
The main purpose of testing DNA samples is to compare them with other samples of DNA to establish information about the suspect or the victim.

TINY SAMPLES

People leave DNA wherever they go. It can be found in flakes of skin that fall to the ground and in sweat left on everything they touch. People sweat more when they are nervous or when they have been eating lots of junk food. Even so, a sample of DNA is sometimes too small to analyze. Now scientists have worked out a way of enlarging the sample by copying it over and over again. This process is called **enhanced DNA**.

IN THE LAB

Samples containing DNA are collected and taken to the lab. Here, the DNA is separated from the cells and analyzed. A computer prints out a copy showing the arrangement of genes. The scientists look for the groups of genes that make the DNA unique. Then they compare the sample with that taken from the suspect.

Winning or losing?
Enhanced DNA on its own has led to the conviction of some criminals, but forensic scientists are worried about how reliable it is. DNA can become damaged or change over time. If a tiny amount of damaged DNA is copied again and again, the faults are copied too. Scientists say that enhanced DNA should only be used alongside other evidence.

Identifying the criminal

While forensic scientists search for evidence, the police look for suspects. First they check whether fingerprints or other evidence found at the crime scene match those of criminals on their files. They ask the victim and witnesses to check photos of known criminals. If they do not recognize anyone in the files, the police then use experts to try to produce a likeness of the criminal, which they show to other police officers and to members of the public.

PRODUCING A LIKENESS

If the criminal has been filmed on **surveillance cameras** (see pages 38–39), the image may be hard to see, but the police have something to start with. Several different systems are also used to produce a likeness by putting together drawings or photos of different parts of the face. The first system, Identikit, was invented by a Los Angeles police officer in 1959. The witness chose a drawing of the eyes, for example, which most resembled the criminal's, then the nose and mouth. In 1970, a new system called Photofit used photos of different features to make a whole face.

Police photo
When a person is arrested he or she is photographed. If that person is later convicted, the photograph is kept on police files.

105-31198

4HDH   4/11

Identifying marks
Tattoos and other marks, such as scars and moles, cannot easily be changed and are useful for identifying people.

IMPROVING THE IMAGE

The problem with Identikit and Photofit was that the photos did not look real. In the 1970s, computers were used to produce E-fit, a system that can bend and stretch the features to make them closer to those the victim or witness recognizes. In the 2000s, a study in the United Kingdom found that people remember and recognize a face if some of the main features are caricatured. This means they are slightly exaggerated.

Breaking through

Criminals on the run try to avoid being recognized by the police by changing their appearance. They may dye their hair or grow a beard. Some use plastic surgery to change, for example, the shape of their nose. This makes it harder for computers to match the person to existing photos. However, there are some aspects of a face, such as the distance between the eyes, that cannot be changed. New systems use these aspects to identify people.

Chapter three: Identifying the weapon

When a criminal uses a weapon, the police must find it and link it to him or her. It may have been abandoned at the crime scene, or it may have been thrown away nearby. If the weapon is missing, forensic scientists have to deduce all they can about the weapon so that the police can trace it.

CARTRIDGE CASES

If the gun is missing, police look for **cartridge cases** and bullets to help them identify the gun. When a trigger is pulled, gunpowder explodes and blasts a bullet down the barrel of the gun. In most guns, including machine guns and rifles, the gunpowder and bullet are packaged together in a cartridge. When the bullet is fired, the cartridge falls to the ground. Each type of gun has its own type of cartridge, and thus can be identified by that cartridge.

Damaged by bullets
Scientists examine the holes left in objects by bullets to help determine the type of gun used at a crime scene.

BULLET CLUES

Different types of guns use different bullets, so a bullet can identify the type of gun used. More than that, however, a bullet can identify the actual gun used. This is how it works. The inside of a barrel has spiral grooves, which make the bullet spin and travel more accurately. The grooves leave a faint pattern, called **rifling**, scratched onto the bullet. The machines that make the grooves in the gun become worn so that each gun leaves the factory with a slightly different pattern of grooves. The gun then scratches a unique pattern on the bullet, and this can be used to identify the gun.

In the ring

Professor Victor Balthazard (1852–1950) was a criminologist working in Paris. He was the first to realize that every gun makes its own rifling marks. He used this knowledge in 1912 to convict a man named Guillotin of murder. Balthazard fired Guillotin's gun in court and photographed the bullet. He then showed the photo to the court along with a photo of the fatal bullet. He showed that the rifling patterns on each bullet matched.

Weapons search

Police divers search for weapons, which may have been thrown into the water. They scour the bottom of lakes and rivers.

Gun crime

Two main types of guns are used in gun crime – long guns and handguns. Long guns include rifles and shotguns. They have a long barrel, which makes them accurate over a long distance. They are held and operated using two hands. Handguns are held in one hand and include pistols and revolvers. They are easy to hide but are less accurate than a rifle. This means that the criminal has to get closer to the victim to shoot him or her.

Bullets and cartridges
The long objects in this photograph are cartridges. Most cartridges are made of metal, but some are made of cardboard. The bullets are the smaller objects in the image.

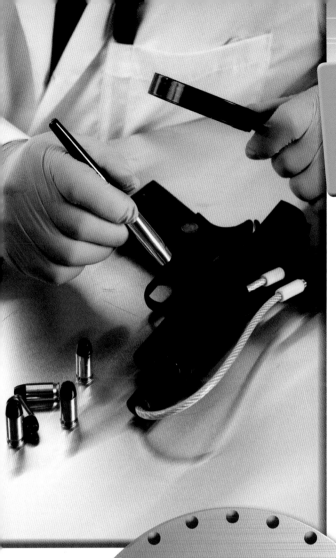

Looking for clues
A forensic scientist examines a gun for fingerprints and traces of gunpowder left behind when the gun was fired.

LINKING BULLETS TO GUNS

In some crimes, more than one kind of gun is used, or there is a gun battle between different people. In this case, investigators are faced with many different cartridges and bullets. They have to work out how many guns were involved and which bullet was fired from which type of gun. Then they try to reconstruct where each of the gunmen stood.

RECONSTRUCTING THE CRIME

Forensic scientists look at where each bullet was found. They look for bullets that may have wounded a person and then ricocheted in another direction. Sometimes a bullet stops inside the victim's body, but sometimes it passes right through.

The pathologist measures the angles at which the bullet entered and left the body. Investigators then use the information to work out where the shooter was standing in relation to the victim when the gun was fired. Scientists also look for nicks, craters and any other signs of bullet damage. They try to trace the path of the bullet backwards to give the position and angle of the gun from which it was fired.

Winning or losing?

Forensic scientists would like the rifling pattern of every gun to be registered before it leaves the factory. This would help them trace a bullet that is fired during a crime back to its gun. Other people argue that such a register would not be of much help because criminals can buy guns overseas and, so, many guns already exist.

Sharp and blunt instruments

Wounds tell investigators a lot about the weapons used by an attacker. Gunshot wounds are easy to recognize, while a knife produces a deep cut. **Blunt instruments** could be any heavy object, from a cricket bat to a brick. They cause bruises and broken bones. An attacker often hits the victim's head, which can fracture the skull and injure the brain.

STAB WOUNDS

When someone is stabbed, forensic scientists can work out several things from the wound or wounds. The size and nature of the wound reveals the size and type of blade. These may suggest a particular type of knife, so scientists can tell the police what to search for. The position of the wound shows whether the attacker was behind or in front of the victim. The angle of the wound shows if the attacker stabbed down or forwards.

Examining the handle
Investigators dust the handle of a weapon found at a crime scene to look for the criminal's fingerprints.

1

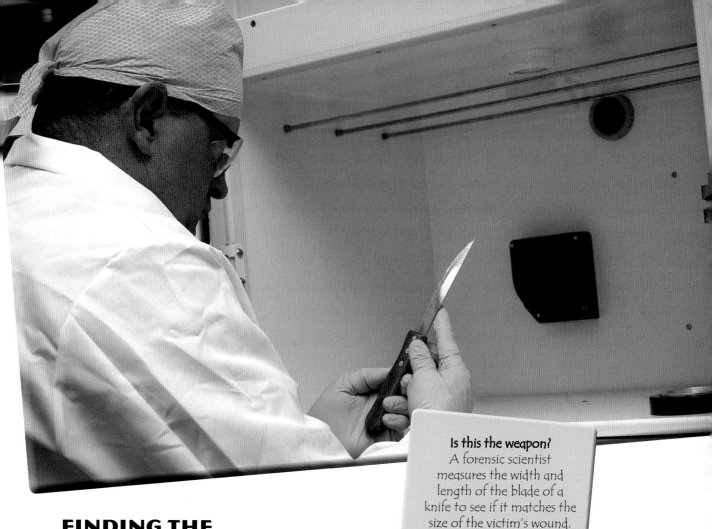

FINDING THE WEAPON

It is harder to link a particular knife or blunt instrument to an attack than it is to link a gun. However, if the weapon is found and examined, it may hold valuable evidence to link it to the crime. Tiny traces of the victim's blood, skin or hair may stick to the weapon, proving that it was the one used. If the weapon has been abandoned, the fingerprints or DNA of the attacker may still be on the handle.

Winning or losing?

Is the level of crime getting worse or are the police managing to reduce it? In 2012, there were around 1.9 million violent crimes committed in England and Wales. This total is 13 per cent lower than it was in 2007. Since then it has continued to fall. In 2014, the total was 1.3 million – its lowest levels in over 30 years. Knives and other sharp implements were the most common homicide weapons.

Databases

At one time, criminals would carry out an armed robbery in one city and then escape from the police by crossing the border into a different county. Today everything has changed. Now police forces pass on the details of crimes to their colleagues in other regions. Television networks also broadcast details of crimes and criminals across the nation, so that the public can pass on information that could help the police.

Computer power
Large computers such as these allow police to store huge amounts of information and share it with other agencies.

COMPUTER FILES

The police store information about crimes on computer files. They have computer programmes that can quickly match fingerprints and DNA. Facial recognition software matches photos, even when the person has changed his or her appearance. The details of guns, bullets and other weapons are also stored on computers. Information that is in the form of a computer file is easy to copy and send to other forces elsewhere.

SHARING INFORMATION

As computers and computer software have developed, law enforcement agencies have been able to share more information. They have set up **databases** such as NIBIN and, in the United Kingdom, the National Ballistics Intelligence Service (NABIS). Ballistics is the study of the effects on the gun and bullet when it is fired. The NABIS database shares data about gun crimes to all British law enforcement agencies.

WORLDWIDE SHARING

Information is not only shared with other agencies and regions, some of it is shared internationally. Interpol is an organization that helps police forces in 190 different countries to work together to solve crimes. Other organizations cover crimes across the United Kingdom and other areas.

In the ring

The National Integrated Ballistic Information Network (NIBIN) stores information about bullets and guns involved in crimes throughout the United States. The system was enlarged and improved after two snipers were convicted in 2002 of murdering 10 people in the Washington area. The gunmen shot people at random as they were doing everyday things, such as shopping. If the bullets could have been matched to an earlier murder in Alabama, the gunmen could have been arrested much sooner.

Types of guns
There are many different types of handgun. This is a pistol, which means that the bullet is held in the barrel.

Chapter four: Evidence, not proof

Some types of evidence can connect a suspect to the scene of a crime, but do not prove that they carried out the crime. This is called **circumstantial evidence.** For example, gravel found in the tyre tread of a suspect's car may match the gravel in the driveway of the house where a body was found. The match shows that the suspect could have been there, but not that he was there when the crime took place.

Clues in treads
Tyres leave tread marks in sand and mud. Some of the sand may stick in the grooves between the treads.

MATCHING EVIDENCE

Fragments of paint, soil or sand are not like fingerprints and DNA. If they match similar fragments at the scene of a crime they show that a link is possible but not certain. The fragment may have come from somewhere else. Tins of paint are sold to many people and the same kind of gravel, sand and even soil can be found in many different places. However, if several things are found to match, it makes the evidence stronger.

SUPPORTING OTHER EVIDENCE

Circumstantial evidence can support other evidence collected against a suspect. The lawyer defending the suspect has to come up with an alternative explanation for the fragments being found on the suspect. Particular chemicals, such as nitroglycerin, can show a link to explosives, but not always. In 1975, six Irishmen were convicted of making bombs after nitroglycerin was found on their hands. In 1990, however, the men won an appeal and were released when it was shown that the chemical could have come from a deck of playing cards.

Button links
A button found at the crime scene may match the buttons on a suspect's coat, but it does not prove that he is the criminal.

Winning or losing?

In 2000, Barry George was convicted of murdering TV star Jill Dando. Police had found several pieces of circumstantial evidence against him. The strongest was a speck of gunpowder on George that matched that in the victim's hair. The jury convicted George, but his lawyer appealed. He argued that the same gunpowder is used in many guns. George was acquitted.

Fibres of cloth

Criminals may take care to wear gloves so that they do not leave fingerprints, and to wipe their feet so that they do not leave particles of dirt. It is much harder for them to guard against leaving behind, or picking up, small **fibres** of cloth. Cloth is soft and tiny fibres easily rub off if touched.

TINY FIBRES

Cloth is made by weaving two threads of yarn together. The yarn may be wool, cotton or an artificial material, such as nylon or polyester. Some yarns are a mixture of materials. Small fibres of material are twisted or spun together to form the yarn.

While the yarn itself is strong, small fibres easily break off. They may be large enough to see under a magnifying glass, or they may be so small that they only show up if examined under a powerful microscope.

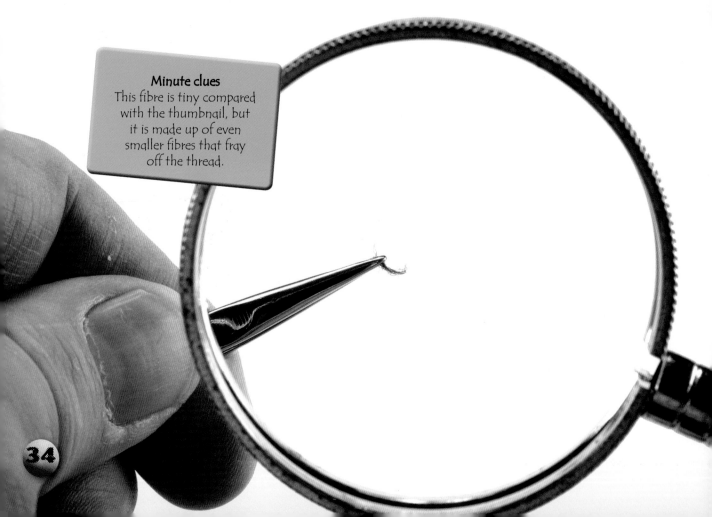

Minute clues
This fibre is tiny compared with the thumbnail, but it is made up of even smaller fibres that fray off the thread.

HOW STRONG IS THE LINK?

Fibres are circumstantial evidence, but sometimes they can provide a strong link between a suspect and the crime. If a fibre of denim is found at a crime scene, it could have come from many sources. However, a fibre of the victim's woollen top found on a suspect makes the link more likely, particularly if it is supported by other evidence. A button found at the crime scene is stronger evidence if the suspect's coat has a button missing.

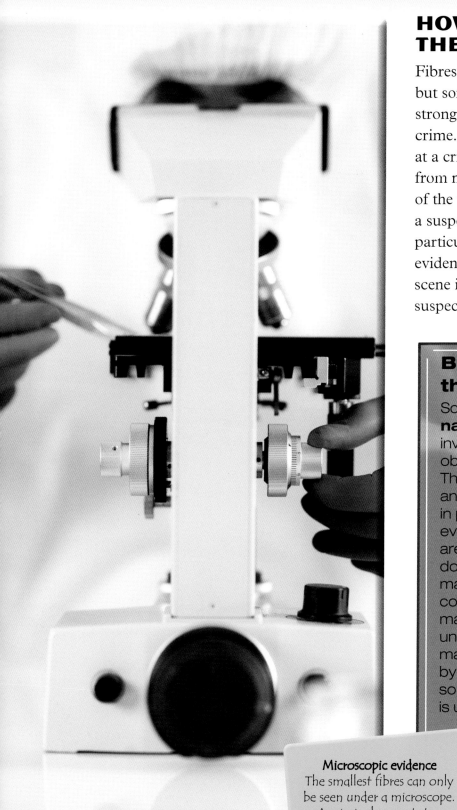

Microscopic evidence
The smallest fibres can only be seen under a microscope. A criminal cannot stop fibres being transferred to or from his or her clothes.

Breaking through

Scientists have used **nanotechnology** to invent a way of tracking objects and materials. They are called taggants and they can be used in paper, clothing and even liquids. Taggants are almost invisible and do not affect the way the material is used. They contain an electronic marker, which is like a unique fingerprint. The marker can be detected by an electronic reader, so that the fibre or object is uniquely identified.

Chapter five: Catching the criminal

Criminals usually flee from the crime scene and try to hide from the police. Science has developed several ways of tracking them. Helicopters search for and follow people on the ground. Criminals think they are safely out of sight, but are they? Police can use dogs and **infrared** cameras to track them. CCTV cameras also help the police to detect and find criminals.

SNIFFER DOGS

A dog's sense of smell is 1,000 times more sensitive than a human's and dogs are easy to train. Dogs are trained to pick up and track the smell of people. Sniffer dogs are trained to recognize particular smells, such as illegal drugs and explosives. They are used to prevent crimes before they even occur.

Smelling trouble
At airports, sniffer dogs are used to detect illegal substances hidden in baggage or carried by people on their bodies.

INFRARED CAMERAS

Police helicopters use infrared cameras to catch people at night, or hidden out of sight in doorways, for example, or under thick bushes. The cameras react to heat in the form of infrared rays, in the same way that other cameras react to light. A living body radiates heat, which the camera picks up and records.

Chasing criminals
Police helicopters are also used during the daytime to track down criminals trying to escape on the ground.

Breaking through
Sniffer dogs sometimes get bored and they also need breaks. Scientists are working on a robot that can detect smells as well as dogs can. The robot is called the cargo-screening ferret, and it has sensors that glow when smells are detected. So far, however, the robots cannot match the dogs!

CCTV cameras

CCTV stands for closed-circuit television. It consists of cameras that relay film straight to computer screens, where it is monitored and stored. In a shop, the camera films parts of the shop the shopkeeper cannot see, and relays it to a screen. In shopping centres, parking lots and other public places the cameras relay pictures to a control room.

Staying in control
Information from speed cameras is shown on computer screens in the control room, allowing police to react quickly to crimes.

HOW THE POLICE USE CCTV

Other than traffic offences, police mainly use CCTV footage to help solve crimes. They ask petrol stations, shops and any other organizations with cameras to check the film recorded around the time of the crime to see if either the suspect or the victim appears on it.

When a shop is burgled, the criminals are often caught on the shop's CCTV. Robbers know this and wear hoods or cover their faces. The main problem with cameras, however, are that the cameras are sometimes switched off and criminals often try to destroy them to avoid being recorded.

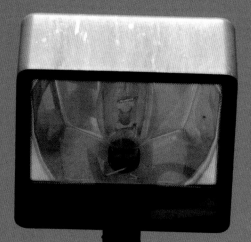

Winning or losing?

Do CCTV and other surveillance cameras make people safer, or are they an intrusion of privacy? Police use listening devices and mobile phone records to track suspects and criminals, but cameras record everyone. Crime rates usually drop in areas that have CCTV cameras, but do the burglars and other criminals simply move elsewhere?

TRACKING NUMBER PLATES

Street and motorway cameras are particularly useful when they are linked to Automatic Number Plate Recognition (ANPR) software, which reads vehicle number plates. The software is linked to a computer database which instantly finds the name and address of the owner. The information is fed into the system so that computer screens in the control room signal when the car is picked up by those cameras. ANPR allows the police to track a vehicle without having to give chase in a police car.

Caught on camera
Cameras attached to posts and the walls of buildings can record what is happening 24 hours a day, every day.

Catching the forgers

Anything that is valuable can be forged, or copied, and passed off as the real thing. One of the most obvious things to forge is money itself, but the companies that print banknotes make this as difficult as possible. Some banknotes include a **hologram** and a strip of metallic thread amongst many other devices. Even so, forgers can produce notes that are very hard to spot.

Printing money
Banknotes are designed to be difficult to forge. Many of the anti-forgery devices are embedded in the way it is printed.

FORGED DOCUMENTS

Important personal documents such as passports, birth certificates and other identity documents are needed to travel to other countries, open a bank account and do many other things. Criminals use forged identity documents to hide their true identities from the police. People from other countries may use forged documents to enter the country. Ordinary people cannot tell the difference, but computer software can!

Real or fake?
Criminals mimic popular
designer brands when they
counterfeit goods such as
sunglasses or handbags.

Breaking through

New technology has been developed to detect fake passports. First issued in 2006, **biometric passports**, or e-passports, use a small, electronic chip that is embedded in the back cover. This chip contains unique physical details that cannot be changed, such as the iris of your eye. Biometric passports enable officials to check the identity of travellers and are very difficult and expensive to forge.

DESIGNER GOODS OR COUNTERFEIT?

People pay large sums of money for goods that carry designer labels, such as jeans and sunglasses. Some people copy the goods but use cheaper materials. Counterfeit goods may be sold cheaply, but others are passed off as the real thing with an expensive price tag. Other criminals record CDs and DVDs to sell cheaply. Everyone involved in producing the originals loses money, including the artists. Police search for counterfeit goods, then seize and dispose of them.

The fight continues: Is science winning?

The battle between criminals and the police changes constantly. As police and forensic scientists find better ways to detect and prevent crime, criminals simply change their methods. Mobile phones used to be an easy target for thieves, but now a phone can be disabled so quickly by the phone company it is not worth stealing. However, new technologies open up new possible illegal activities, continuing the constant fight against crime.

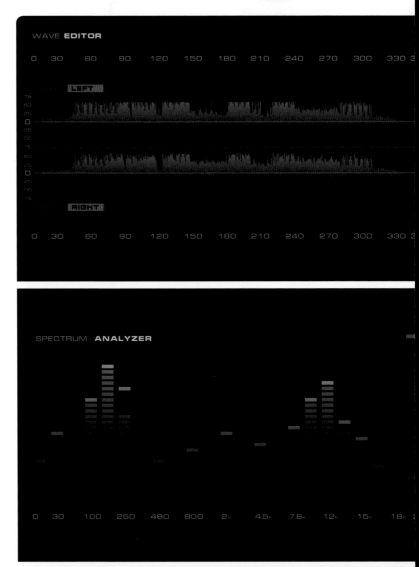

Analyzing sound waves
Sound labs use spectral analysis to examine different aspects of sound. It can also be used to analyze light and thus detect forgeries.

Breaking through

As computer software becomes better at copying and changing sounds and photos, scientists have looked for better ways to spot computer forgeries.

Bispectral analysis looks at separate wavelengths in sound to detect unnatural patterns or changes that indicate a forgery. The software can tell whether the tape of a person's voice is really the voice of the person it claims to be.

Biometric passport
The front cover of a biometric passport is printed with a special symbol to show that it contains an electronic chip.

OPPORTUNITIES FOR NEW CRIMES

Cybercrime is any crime that involves the internet. For example, bank robbers used to go into a bank and demand money, but today some bank robbers break into the bank's computer systems and move large sums of money into their own accounts. Other cybercriminals steal a person's identity and then use it to spend large amounts of their victim's money.

NEWS WAYS OF DETECTING

Police forces use new technology too. Phone calls and texts sent by mobile phone can be traced by the police. Messages and photographs left on social networking sites are easy for the police to access. When protests or riots are being planned or in progress, police check Twitter to pick up useful information. One of the advantages for criminals, and one of the problems for police, is that a criminal can commit a crime in another country without leaving home.

The crime story

1813
Mathieu Orfila, a Spanish chemist, publishes a book about how to detect different poisons. He developed tests for detecting blood and was one of the first people to practise forensic medicine.

1856
Sir William Herschel, recognizing that fingerprints are unique, allows thumbprints to be used on documents in place of written signatures.

1860s
The first tests for detecting the presence of blood are developed in both the Netherlands and Germany.

1880s
Alphonse Bertillon becomes the first forensic scientist to photograph crime scenes before they are disturbed.

1893
Austrian professor of criminal law Hans Gross publishes a book which brings together all the different sources of evidence used to solve a crime.

1912
Professor Victor Balthazard uses rifling to match Guillotin's gun to the bullet used to murder a man called Houssard.

1920s
Calvin Goddard, a firearms expert, develops a comparison microscope so that the rifling marks on two bullets can be easily compared.

1932
The FBI's crime laboratory is established.

1953
James Watson and Francis Crick discover the structure of DNA, with the help of X-ray photographs taken by Rosalind Franklin.

1963
President John F. Kennedy is assassinated. His assassin, Lee Harvey Oswald, is identified by a palm print left on the rifle.

1980
The FBI first uses computers to match fingerprints.

1984
Dr Alec Jeffreys discovers a way of identifying a person from their DNA, called DNA profiling or DNA fingerprinting.

1988
DNA profiling is used for the first time in a British court.

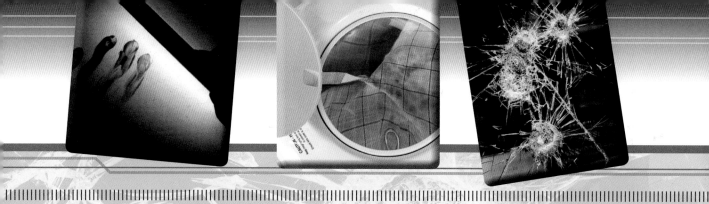

1901
Karl Landsteiner discovers that there are four main blood groups in humans.

1892
Sir Francis Galton publishes a book which describes different fingerprint patterns and shows that no two fingerprints are identical.

1903
New York State Prison begins to use fingerprints to identify criminals.

1908
President Theodore Roosevelt sets up the Federal Bureau of Investigation (FBI), the detective agency that covers the whole of the United States.

1910
Edmond Locard sets up the first forensic laboratory in Lyon, France. His statement that "every contact leaves a trace" is one of the basic ideas of forensic science.

1992
Drugfire, an automatic system for comparing rifling marks on bullets, is developed for the FBI.

1995
The UK's National DNA Database, a database of DNA profiles, is set up.

2001
England and Wales set up computerized searches of the National Automated Fingerprints Identification System (NAFIS).

2009
England and Wales set up the National Ballistics Intelligence Service (NABIS), which stores forensic information from all guns and bullets.

2013
The National Crime Agency is set up in the United Kingdom to fight serious and organized crime, both nationally and internationally.

Glossary

assassin person who kills or tries to kill someone for political or monetary reasons

assault physical attack

biometric passport passport embedded with a computer chip containing unique personal data

bispectral analysis method of analyzing sounds or light to detect forgeries

blunt instrument weapon without sharp points or blades

cartridge case casing that contains a bullet and a powder that ignites and explodes to fire the bullet

CCTV the letters stand for closed-circuit television, which is equipment that includes one or more cameras linked to television or computer screens

circumstantial evidence evidence that is linked to events surrounding a crime

contaminated polluted by something that happened after the crime

counterfeit something that is fake or forged

database collection of information stored on a computer

DNA chains of genes that control how all living things grow and function

enhanced DNA large amount of DNA produced by copying a small amount of DNA over and over again

evidence object, such as a weapon, fingerprint or photograph, which is related to a crime

fibre tiny thread

forensic scientist scientist who helps police and other investigators to solve crimes

gene tiny part of a living thing that is passed from parents to offspring. The collection of genes inherited by the offspring are unique.

hacking breaking into a computer system in order to change or steal information

hologram photograph or motif made by lasers

infrared form of energy that produces heat

luminol chemical that glows when it is in contact with blood

nanotechnology technology that uses tiny particles called atoms – the smallest part of a chemical

nitroglycerin oily liquid that explodes easily

pathologist scientist who specializes in things that go wrong in the human body. A forensic pathologist is an expert on the effect of crime on the human body.

rifling grooves inside the barrel of a gun that leave a unique pattern on a bullet fired from the gun

sniper shooter who hides himself or herself before firing at a person or people

surveillance camera camera that is usually attached to a recording device, used to observe an area

witness person who sees or hears a particular event, such as a crime

Find out more

BOOKS

Crime-fighting Devices (Sci-Hi), Robert Snedden
(Raintree, 2012)

Crime Scene Clues (Zoom In On...), Richard Spilsbury
(Wayland, 2015)

Solving Crimes in the Lab (Forensic Science), Carol Ballard
(Franklin Watts, 2010)

True Stories of Crime & Detection, Gill Harvey
(Usborne Children's Books, 2015)

WEBSITES

For fun fingerprinting activities, including facts and worksheets, go to:
www.creative-chemistry.org.uk/activities/fingerprinting.htm

This interactive game gives you various options to follow to solve a crime:
**www.museevirtuel-virtualmuseum.ca/sgc-cms/expositions-exhibitions/
detective-investigator/en/game/index.php**

To find out more about DNA profiling and how it can solve crimes, go to:
**www.sciencemuseum.org.uk/WhoAmI/FindOutMore/Yourgenes/
Whydoscientistsstudygenes.aspx**

Index